INTRODUCTION

LOOK AT YOUR BODY! Or rather you should ask yourself how can you look at your body? Your eyes form an important part of your ability to experience the outside world. Your ears, nose, tongue and the skin that covers your body are also involved. All of these parts are riddled with tiny sensors that are bombarded throughout each day with different types of information – colours, shapes, smells, tastes, sounds and contact. There are also millions of tiny sensors inside your body, checking everything from the position of your head and limbs to the levels of different chemicals in your blood. All of this information is sent to your brain, which sifts it, sorts it and analyses it to give you a clear picture of the world around you and inside your body.

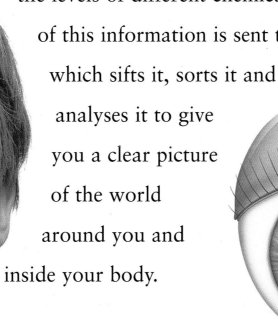

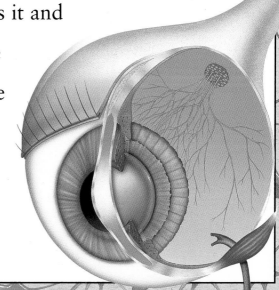

SENSING THE WORLD

AN ANIMAL'S SENSES are adapted and tuned to its surroundings. They help it detect what is important for its survival – locating food, detecting danger, seeking shelter and finding a mate. These senses include the five that you have – hearing, sight, taste, touch and smell – as well as a few that you haven't.

Some creatures may have to live in conditions where a human's senses would be almost useless. As such, they have developed different ways of surviving in their environment. For instance, bats can locate their prey in complete darkness using high-pitched squeaks, while some snakes can "see" the heat of a living body!

4

DANGER BELOW
The trapdoor spider (below) lurks hidden in its burrow. However, it has laid fine silk threads on the ground around the entrance, and holds the ends of the threads in its legs. As a small creature, such as a beetle, touches these threads, it alerts the spider who then rushes out to catch its victim.

RUMBLE IN THE JUNGLE
Elephants (right) roam the countryside, sometimes more than 1 km (0.6 miles) away from other members of their herd. They keep in touch using extremely deep rumbling noises. These are so low-pitched that humans cannot hear them. But the elephants can, and use these rumblings to meet, greet or warn other elephants.

LOOK AT YOUR BODY
SENSES

STEVE PARKER

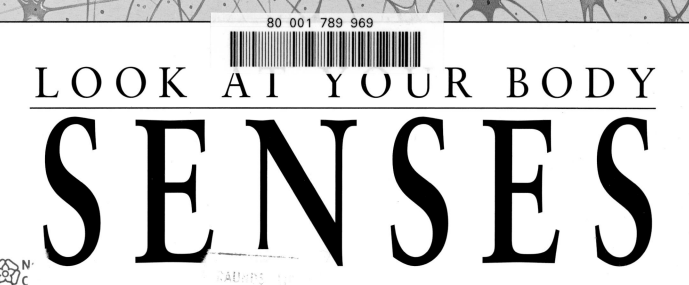

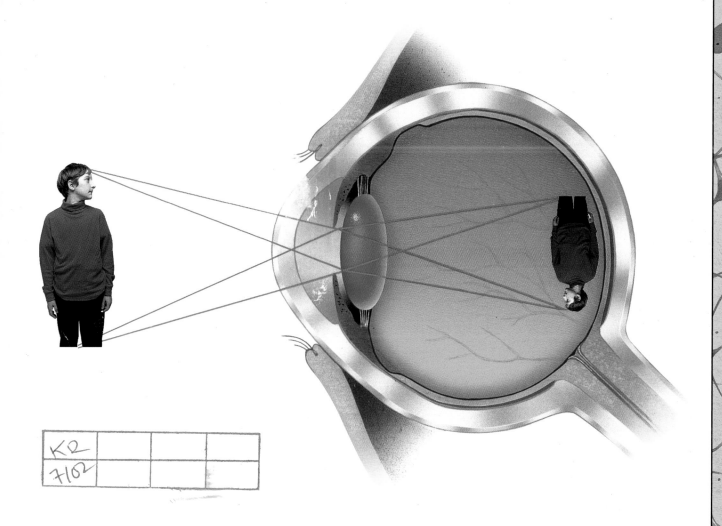

Franklin Watts
London • Sydney

This edition published
in 2001
© Aladdin Books Ltd
1996
All rights reserved
Designed and
produced by
Aladdin Books Ltd
28 Percy Street
London W1P 0LD

First published in
Great Britain in 1996
by
Franklin Watts
96 Leonard Street
London EC2A 4XD

ISBN 0 7496 2540 6 (hb)
ISBN 0 7496 4098 7 (pbk)

A catalogue record
for this book is
available from the
British Library.

Printed in U.A.E.

Editor Jon Richards

Design
David West
Children's Book Design
Designer
Rob Perry

Illustrators
Ian Thompson and
Mark Iley
Picture research
Brooks Krikler Research
Consultant
Dr R Levene MB.BS,
DCH, DRCOG

Steve Parker has
written over 100
books for
children, many
of those concerning
human anatomy and
physiology.

CONTENTS

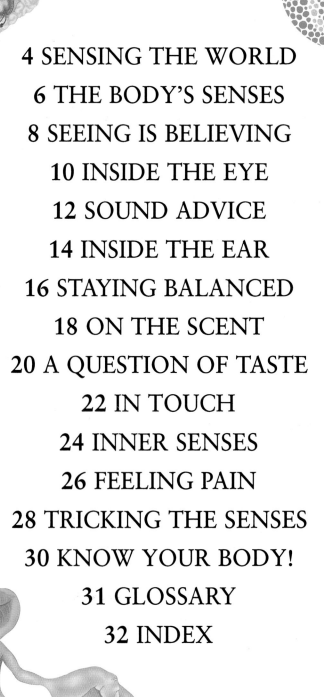

High-pitched squeaks

Echoes

SQUEAKS IN THE SKY
Bats usually fly in complete darkness. They catch their prey of moths and flies by making bursts of very shrill squeaks which are so high-pitched that humans cannot hear them. These sounds bounce off objects and the bat listens for the returning echoes to pinpoint its target (left).

THE FLY'S EYE
A fly's eye is made of hundreds of separate units (above). Each of these detects a tiny portion of a scene. These small parts then get put together by the fly's brain to get the whole picture.

GLOW IN THE DARK
The pit viper (above) can locate and catch prey, such as a mouse, even in total darkness. To do this, it uses special pit organs under each eye. These can detect the heat, in the form of infra-red light (see page 8), given off by the body of a living animal.

Membrane holding smell detectors

WORLD OF SMELLS
The typical dog has a very good sense of smell. Inside its nose (left), the tiny smell detectors cover a membrane about 50 times greater than those in our own nose. A dog's sense of smell may be more than 1,000 times more sensitive than that of a human.

THE BODY'S SENSES

WE ARE OFTEN TOLD that the human body has just the five senses of sight, hearing, smell, taste and touch. However, this view is slightly misleading. The body has, in fact, dozens of other senses. Many are internal sensing mechanisms that monitor position, pressure, pain and the levels of substances such as blood sugar (see pages 24-25) and carbon dioxide.

However, all sensory parts, or sense organs, work in the same basic way. They change information that comes from the outside world or your own body, such as light reflecting off an object, or the positions of your various limbs, into tiny electrical pulses called nerve signals, and send these to the brain for decoding and analysis.

6

(see pages 24-25)

BALANCE
Balance is not a single sense. It is a process that is happening all the time and involves many sensors in the body. It is linked with hearing because it involves detectors inside the ears.

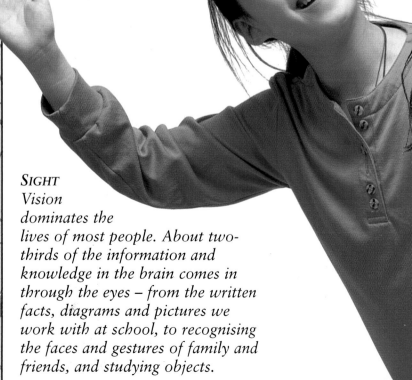

SIGHT
Vision dominates the lives of most people. About two-thirds of the information and knowledge in the brain comes in through the eyes – from the written facts, diagrams and pictures we work with at school, to recognising the faces and gestures of family and friends, and studying objects.

HEARING

Hearing is usually the second most important sense, after sight. We learn to listen so that we can take in knowledge, communicate with others and detect any approaching danger.

TOUCH

This sense is much more complex than it may seem. The skin contains millions of tiny sensors that can detect not only physical contact, but also texture, heat, cold, vibrations, levels of pressure, itching, soreness, physical discomfort and pain.

TASTE AND SMELL

These two senses are physically separate and work independently, sending two sets of nerve signals to the brain. However, they are frequently experienced in the brain at the same time when we sense the odours and flavours of foods and drinks.

SEEING IS BELIEVING

OUR SENSE OF VISION is the one we use and trust the most. It allows us to detect things from a great distance. On a bright, clear day and from a good viewpoint, we can see another human or similar-sized animal, such as a lion, moving over 2 km (1.25 miles) away.

Like our close relations the apes and monkeys, we can see the full spectrum of colours clearly. Our two eyes allow us to judge distances accurately using binocular vision (see below). Estimating distance is also helped by features such as the way colours fade and objects become hazy with distance, and parallax – the relative sizes of objects as they become smaller the further away they get.

LIGHT AND RAYS
Visible light rays are part of a much wider range of waves called the electromagnetic spectrum. This spectrum also includes infra-red and ultraviolet light, gamma rays and X-rays (above).

8

Some people cannot distinguish the full range of colours clearly. The common name for this is colour blindness. Can you see a number on the right? People with normal vision should see the number "8". Inability to see this number may indicate a problem with colour vision.

RIGHT FIELD OF VISION

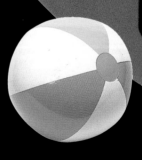

BINOCULAR (STEREOSCOPIC) VISION
Each eye sees an area called its field of vision. These fields overlap in a central area (main picture). Here, both eyes see slightly different views of the same scene. For example, close your right eye and hold up your thumb so that it covers a distant object, such as an apple. Now, without moving your thumb, open your right eye and close your left eye. You will see that the thumb no longer covers the apple (right).

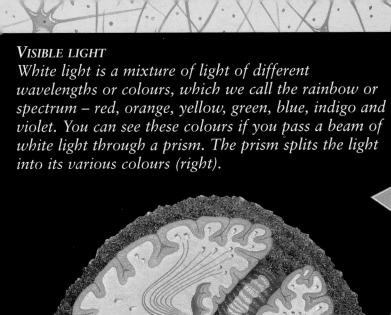

VISIBLE LIGHT

White light is a mixture of light of different wavelengths or colours, which we call the rainbow or spectrum – red, orange, yellow, green, blue, indigo and violet. You can see these colours if you pass a beam of white light through a prism. The prism splits the light into its various colours (right).

Optic nerve

Optic chiasma

Visual cortex

EYES AND BRAIN

The eyes do not really "see". They pick up patterns of light rays, turn them into nerve signals and send these signals along the optic nerves to the brain. The nerves exchange fibres at the optic chiasma in the lower front of the brain, partially combining the signals from left and right eyes. The nerve signals continue to areas on the lower rear surfaces of the brain (above), the left visual cortex and right visual cortex. Here they are analysed and interpreted by the brain, and this is where you "see".

9

LEFT FIELD OF VISION

ON THE SIDE

Animals like zebras (right) have eyes on the sides of their head. This gives them good sideways vision to spot any predators, but poor forward and 3-D sight.

BRIGHT EYES

Too much bright light can damage the eye's delicate interior. Wearing suitable sunglasses (left) can protect against this. They can also reduce glare and protect against the damaging effects of ultraviolet light rays.

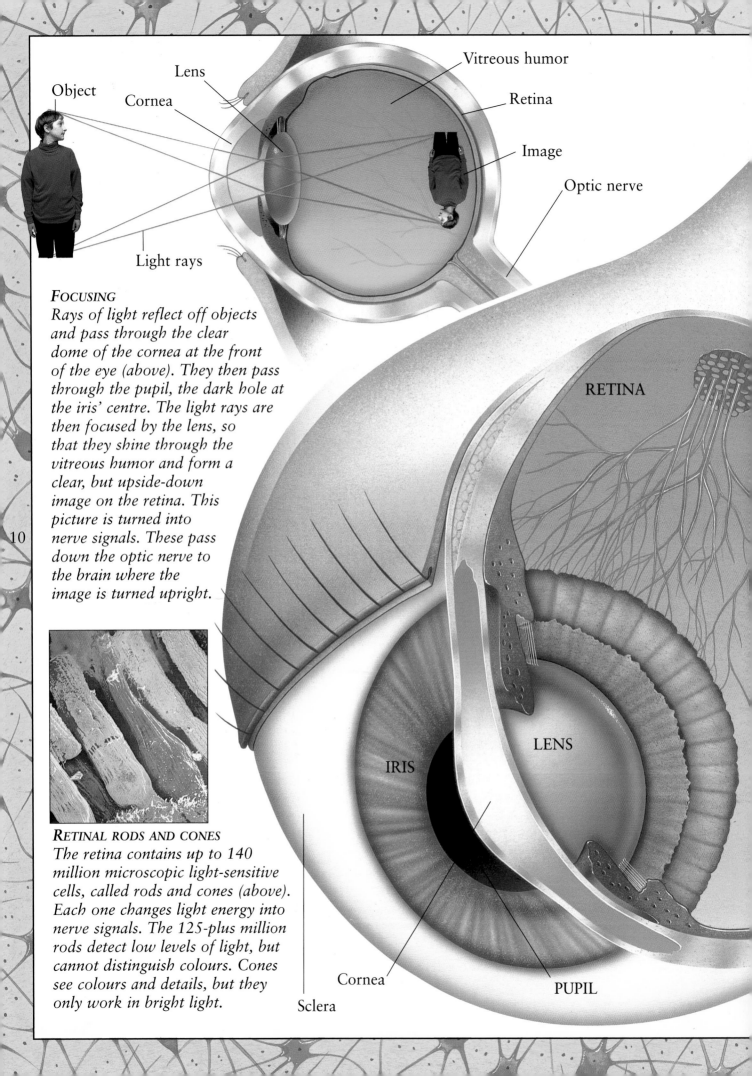

Object

Cornea

Lens

Vitreous humor

Retina

Image

Optic nerve

Light rays

FOCUSING

Rays of light reflect off objects and pass through the clear dome of the cornea at the front of the eye (above). They then pass through the pupil, the dark hole at the iris' centre. The light rays are then focused by the lens, so that they shine through the vitreous humor and form a clear, but upside-down image on the retina. This picture is turned into nerve signals. These pass down the optic nerve to the brain where the image is turned upright.

10

RETINAL RODS AND CONES

The retina contains up to 140 million microscopic light-sensitive cells, called rods and cones (above). Each one changes light energy into nerve signals. The 125-plus million rods detect low levels of light, but cannot distinguish colours. Cones see colours and details, but they only work in bright light.

RETINA

IRIS

LENS

Cornea

PUPIL

Sclera

INSIDE THE EYE

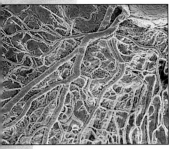

BLOOD VESSELS
The back of the eye is covered by branches of blood vessels (above) which supply the retina with nutrients.

EACH EYEBALL is covered with a tough outer sheath called the sclera, except for the coloured part at the front. This coloured circle on your eye is called the iris. At its centre is the black pupil. The iris changes size to let more or less light through the pupil and into the eye.

Most of the eye's interior is filled with a clear jelly, the vitreous humor. The part that detects light, the retina, lines the rear of the eyeball. This very delicate layer provides the detailed, moving pictures of the world that you experience in your brain.

Cataracts affect millions of people around the world and are a major cause of blindness in less-developed

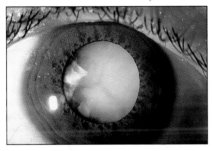

countries. This misting or haziness in the lens (left) obscures sight. As it worsens it can cause total loss of vision. Surgery to remove the misty portion or the whole lens, and insert a plastic artificial version (above) or implant, can drastically improve eyesight.

11

BLOOD
VESSELS

Tear duct

LONG SIGHT
The eye is too small compared with the power of its lens, so the image cannot be focused (right). Convex lenses will focus the image on the retina.

SHORT SIGHT
The eye is too large compared with the focusing power of its lens. Concave lenses diverge the light rays before they reach the eye's own lens.

TEARS
The tear gland makes salty tear fluid. This flows onto the eyeball, where the eyelids wipe it across the surface. It helps remove dust and germs. When we cry (below), we produce a lot of tears.

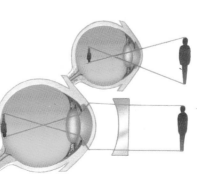

SOUND ADVICE

SOUND WAVES ARE INVISIBLE RIPPLES of high and low air pressure created by objects that vibrate, or shake rapidly to and fro. The height they vibrate to is called their amplitude and this is related to the loudness of the sound. The distance between each wave peak is called the wavelength. This is related to the pitch of the sound. The number of times they vibrate each second is called their frequency, and is measured in hertz (Hz).

Our hearing provides information about objects which are far away, from a lion's roar to the horn of a car. Hearing is also important for communicating with each other through speech and other sounds.

Continued exposure to loud noises can damage the ear's delicate interior (see pages 14-15). People in noisy situations, such as using road drills (right), working near loud machinery or with loud music, should wear ear defenders to prevent this from happening. Prolonged exposure may cause some loss of hearing or even complete deafness. It can also cause tinnitus. This is a constant ringing, buzzing, whistling and other noises in the ear.

12

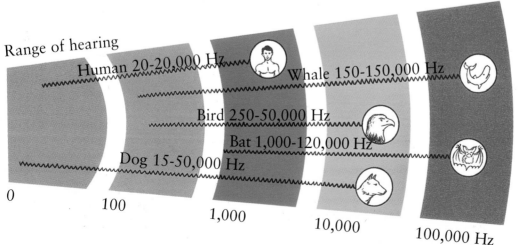

Range of hearing

Human 20-20,000 Hz

Whale 150-150,000 Hz

Bird 250-50,000 Hz

Bat 1,000-120,000 Hz

Dog 15-50,000 Hz

0   100   1,000   10,000   100,000 Hz

ANIMAL HEARING
Many animals can hear sounds far beyond our range of hearing. These include the incredibly high-pitched squeaks bats make to guide their way through the night sky and the clicks and beeps that whales use to communicate (left).

HIGH PITCH
High notes, such as those played on a flute (right), have a short wavelength and a high frequency (see green wave, below).

Loud, high-pitched note

SOUND AND DISTANCE
As sound waves travel out from their source (above right), like the ripples on a pond, their energy decreases the further away they become. This is why sounds get quieter the further away you are from their source. Also, as you move away, the pitch of a sound drops. This is due to the wave's energy loss lowering its frequency.

Rocket lift-off 180 dB

Jet 130 dB

13

Thunder 120 dB

Band 110 dB

Talking 60 dB

Rustling leaves 10 dB

Quiet, low-pitched note

LOW PITCH
Low notes, such as those played by a tuba (right), have a long wavelength and a low frequency (see yellow wave, above).

VOLUME
A sound wave's height is related to its loudness or volume – the larger the height of the wave, the louder the sound (right). The volume, or intensity, is measured in decibels (dB). Most normal conversation is at 60 dB.

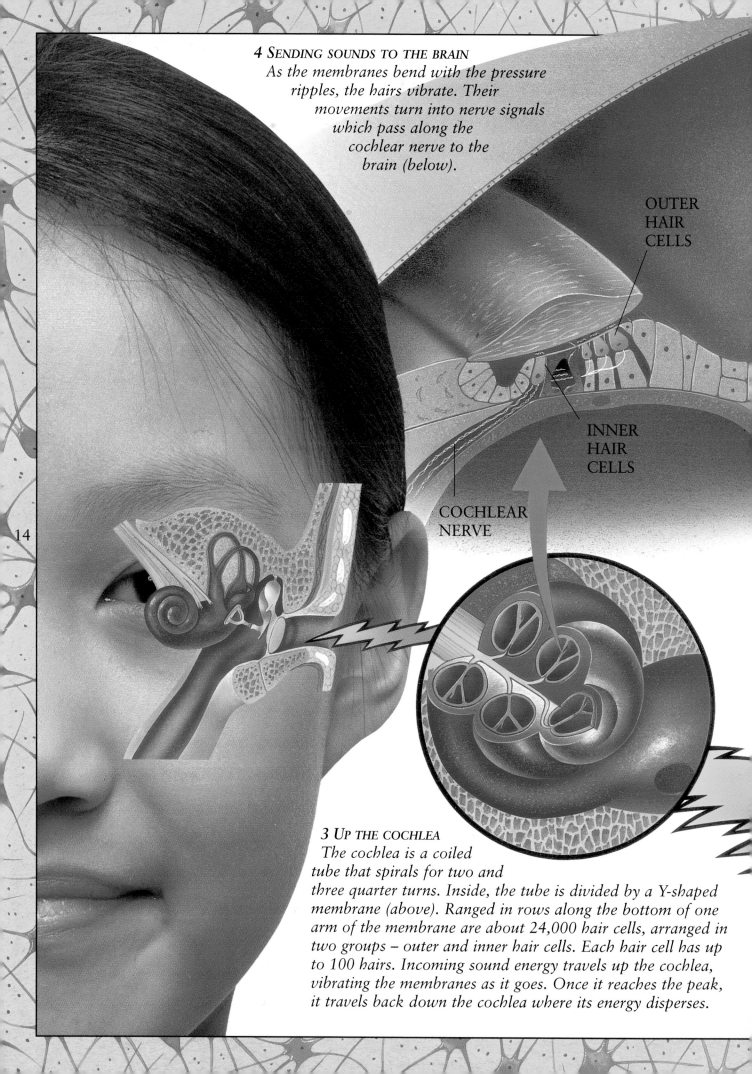

4 SENDING SOUNDS TO THE BRAIN
*As the membranes bend with the pressure
ripples, the hairs vibrate. Their
movements turn into nerve signals
which pass along the
cochlear nerve to the
brain (below).*

OUTER
HAIR
CELLS

INNER
HAIR
CELLS

COCHLEAR
NERVE

14

3 UP THE COCHLEA
*The cochlea is a coiled
tube that spirals for two and
three quarter turns. Inside, the tube is divided by a Y-shaped
membrane (above). Ranged in rows along the bottom of one
arm of the membrane are about 24,000 hair cells, arranged in
two groups – outer and inner hair cells. Each hair cell has up
to 100 hairs. Incoming sound energy travels up the cochlea,
vibrating the membranes as it goes. Once it reaches the peak,
it travels back down the cochlea where its energy disperses.*

INSIDE THE EAR

LIKE ALL OTHER SENSE ORGANS, the ear converts one type of energy – in this case, the energy of sound waves – into tiny electrical nerve signals. This transformation happens deep inside the ear, in the snail-shaped organ of hearing, called the cochlea. This grape-sized part is embedded and protected inside the skull, just behind and below your eye.

The whole of the ear is divided into three main parts – the inner, middle and outer ears. The outer ear is made up of the funnel-shaped piece of flesh that sits on the side of your head and the ear canal. The middle ear consists of the eardrum and the three ear bones. Finally, the inner ear is made up of the cochlea and the cochlear nerve.

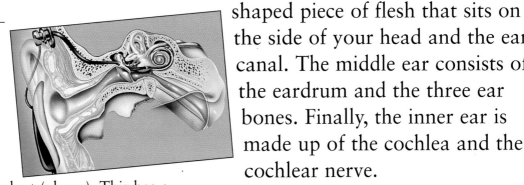

Should the cochlea or ear bones become damaged, hearing may be lost. Doctors can restore hearing by using an artificial implant (above). This has a microphone which converts sounds into electronic pulses. These are sent down a wire into the cochlea, where they stimulate the cochlear nerve.

15

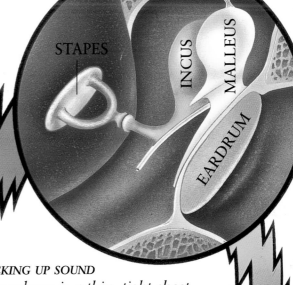

STAPES
INCUS
MALLEUS
EARDRUM

2 INTO THE COCHLEA
The base or foot of the stapes is attached to a thin, flexible part of the cochlear wall. As the stapes tilts and pushes in and out like a piston, it transfers waves or ripples of pressure along the fluid inside the cochlea.

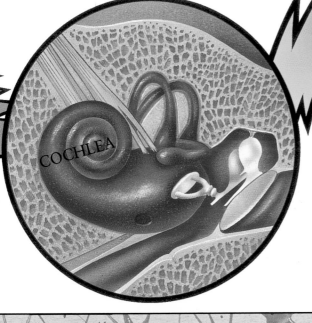

COCHLEA

1 PICKING UP SOUND
The eardrum is a thin, tight sheet of skin-like material. Sound waves bounce off it making it vibrate. These vibrations are passed along the three ear bones, or ossicles; malleus, incus and stapes. The bones pass the vibrations to the cochlea.

STAYING BALANCED

BALANCE IS NOT A SINGLE SENSE. It is a continuous body mechanism that processes inputs from various senses, analyses these in the brain, and sends messages to the muscles.

The inputs come from four main sources.

First are the two sets of sensors found deep inside each ear. Second are the microscopic stretch and strain gauges in the muscles, tendons and joints around the body, called proprioceptors. They allow us to know the position of the head, neck, body and limbs. Third are the eyes, which see verticals and horizontals and so judge the head's angle. Fourth is the skin, which feels touch and pressure according to how gravity pulls down on the body.

SEMICIRCULAR CANALS
In each ear there are three C-shaped, fluid-filled tubes, called semicircular canals. They are at right angles to each other, pointing up-down, side-side and front-back. Whichever way the head moves, fluid swirls inside at least one canal. At one end of each canal is a bulge, the ampulla. Inside, is a jelly-like lump, the crista. This bends as the fluid swirls (left) distorting hairs that project from cells below. These send nerve signals to the brain, telling it about the body's movements.

Semicircular canal

CRISTA

Ampullae

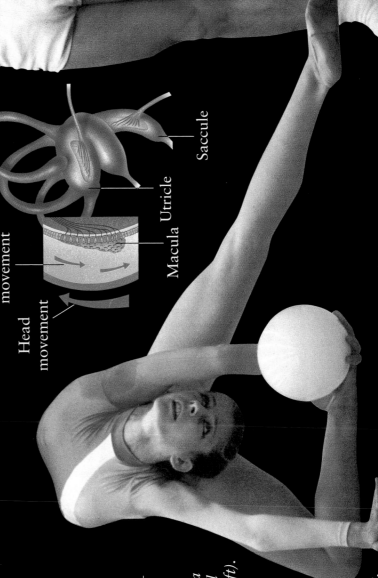

SACCULE AND SACCULE

Near the inner ear's semicircular canals and cochlea are two fluid-filled chambers, the saccule and utricle. Each has a macula, a patch of hair cells with their tips embedded in a jelly-like membrane. The two chambers and their maculae are at right angles. As the head changes position, the fluid drags on the membranes. This pulls on the hairs sticking into the maculae, making their cells generate nerve signals. In this way the utricle and saccule act as sensors for head position and acceleration or deceleration – whether you are standing upright or bent over backwards!

Macula

Saccule

Macula

Utricle

Fluid movement

Head movement

M otion sickness happens when the body is moved in unnatural ways, such as in a boat on a rough sea (above). This swirls the fluids in the inner-ear. The sensors send confusing signals to the brain, which may not add up with what the eyes see and the skin feels. The result is nausea and giddiness, as the brain tries to make sense of the conflicting signals.

SURVIVAL BY BALANCE
A cat seems to have a magical ability to fall safely on all fours (left). In fact it uses the same senses as us, but they work faster and more accurately. As the cat falls, it twists its head level. The rest of the body quickly follows.

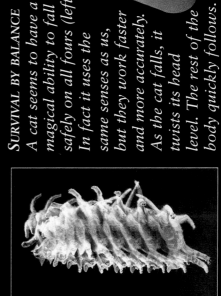

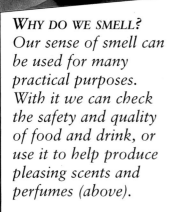

ON THE SCENT

S MELL CAN BE VERY USEFUL to us, helping our survival by detecting the bad scents of things that might be harmful. The nose has developed to detect airborne chemicals, which are called odorants. These smells are carried through the nostrils and into the nasal cavity on the stream of air that you take into your lungs when you breathe.

In the roof of the cavity are two patches of sensitive tissue called the olfactory epithelia, each covering the area of a thumbnail. Together, they contain over 20 million sensory olfactory cells (see opposite) which detect the odorants. However, after about 30 seconds, any scent becomes hard to detect as the nose becomes accustomed to the odour. This is called habituation.

WHY DO WE SMELL?
Our sense of smell can be used for many practical purposes. With it we can check the safety and quality of food and drink, or use it to help produce pleasing scents and perfumes (above).

18

BAD SMELL
Many animals use scent as a way of communicating. The skunk (below) uses a powerful stink to warn off any would-be attackers. Any that don't take the hint may be sprayed with a stinging chemical!

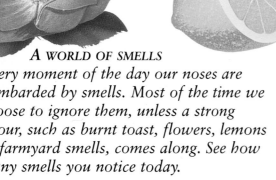

A WORLD OF SMELLS
Every moment of the day our noses are bombarded by smells. Most of the time we choose to ignore them, unless a strong odour, such as burnt toast, flowers, lemons or farmyard smells, comes along. See how many smells you notice today.

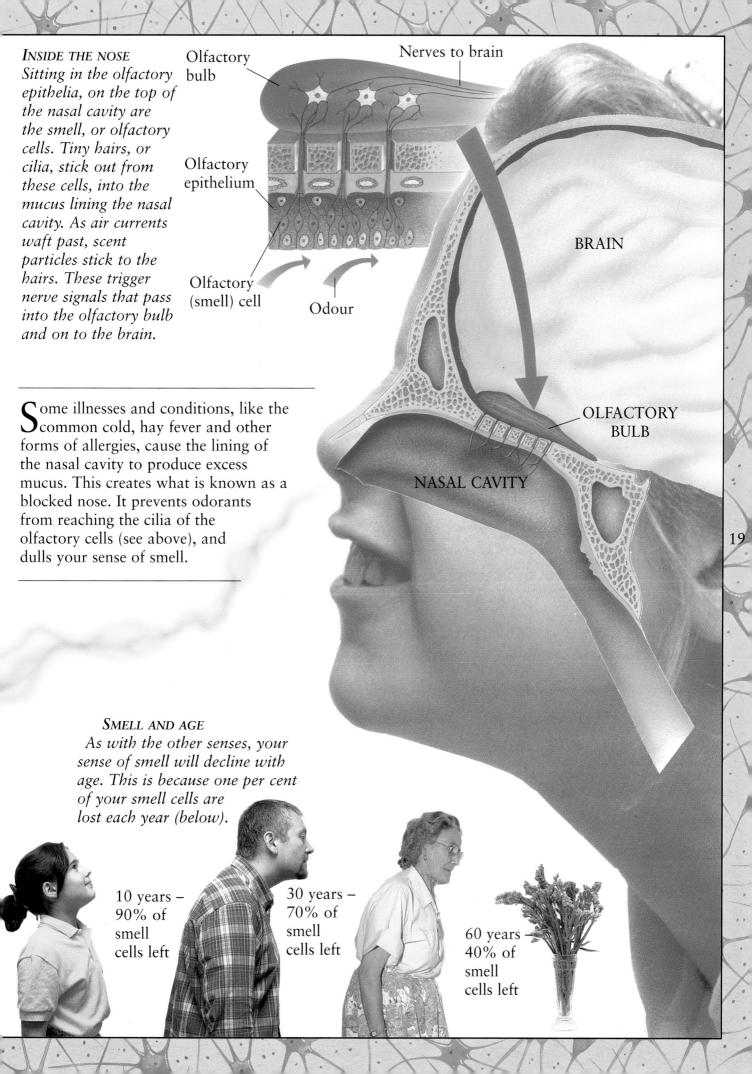

INSIDE THE NOSE
Sitting in the olfactory epithelia, on the top of the nasal cavity are the smell, or olfactory cells. Tiny hairs, or cilia, stick out from these cells, into the mucus lining the nasal cavity. As air currents waft past, scent particles stick to the hairs. These trigger nerve signals that pass into the olfactory bulb and on to the brain.

Olfactory bulb

Nerves to brain

Olfactory epithelium

Olfactory (smell) cell

Odour

BRAIN

OLFACTORY BULB

NASAL CAVITY

Some illnesses and conditions, like the common cold, hay fever and other forms of allergies, cause the lining of the nasal cavity to produce excess mucus. This creates what is known as a blocked nose. It prevents odorants from reaching the cilia of the olfactory cells (see above), and dulls your sense of smell.

19

SMELL AND AGE
As with the other senses, your sense of smell will decline with age. This is because one per cent of your smell cells are lost each year (below).

10 years – 90% of smell cells left

30 years – 70% of smell cells left

60 years – 40% of smell cells left

A QUESTION OF TASTE

BOTH NOSE AND TONGUE detect dissolved chemicals. In the mouth, these usually arrive in the form of flavour molecules from foods and drinks. In fact, it is believed that the multitude of flavours you experience when you eat and drink are based on various combinations of only four basic flavours – sweet, sour, salty and bitter (see opposite).

Originally, our sense of taste probably evolved to warn us about foods that were bad, rotten or poisonous in some way. Then people learned what was good to eat, and how to recognise, cook and flavour foods with a huge variety of sauces, herbs, spices and other substances. Along with progress in agriculture and food storage, this turned eating from a necessity for survival into an enjoyable taste experience.

PAPILLAE
The surface of the tongue is covered with thousands of tiny pimples, called papillae (below left). They give the tongue a bumpy surface and make it rough to help move food around while you chew.

TONGUE NERVES
The tongue is connected to the brain by three cranial nerves (main picture). Two of these deal with the taste sensations, taking the information back to the brain where it can be processed. The third nerve controls the movements of the tongue, helping you talk and chew food.

POISONOUS PLANTS
Your sense of taste can protect you from substances that may be harmful to you if they got inside your body. Many poisonous plants, such as the Yew tree (left), have a bitter taste that will warn you of their dangerous properties.

TASTE BUDS

Taste buds are tiny ball-like clusters of crescent-shaped cells, like segments in a microscopic orange (below). They are set into the surface of the tongue, especially around the sides of the papillae. A tiny opening lets dissolved flavour particles seep onto the hairs at the top of the taste bud.

PAPILLA

Taste bud

Taste hairs

Taste cells

Nerve

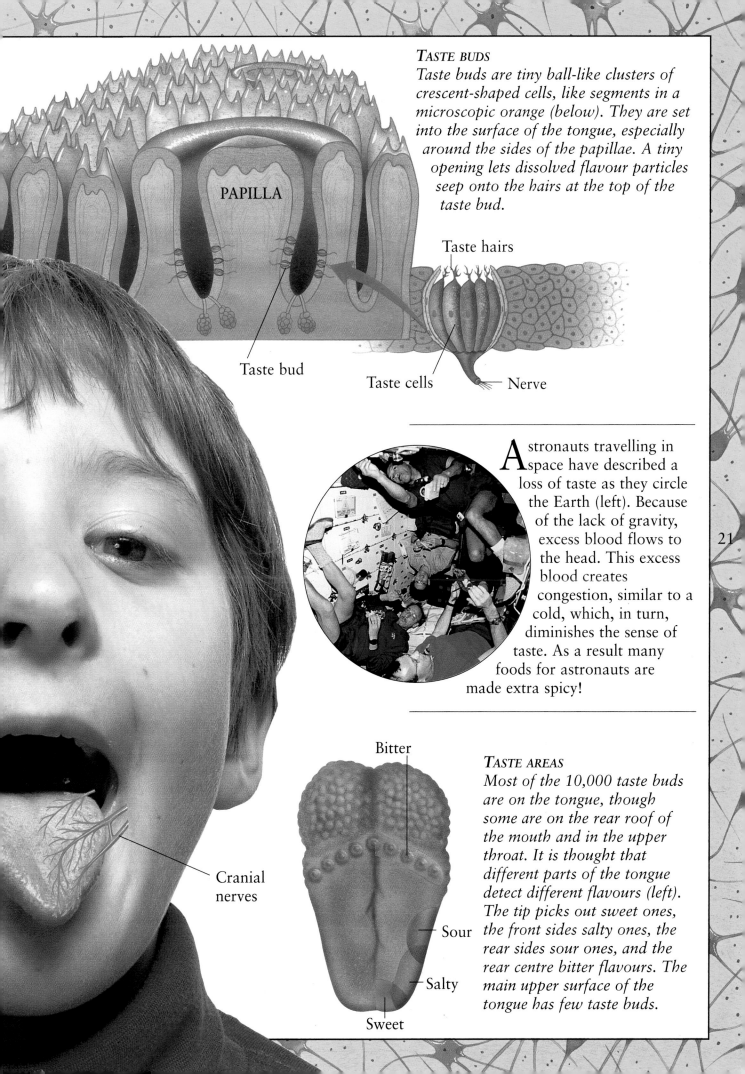

Cranial nerves

Astronauts travelling in space have described a loss of taste as they circle the Earth (left). Because of the lack of gravity, excess blood flows to the head. This excess blood creates congestion, similar to a cold, which, in turn, diminishes the sense of taste. As a result many foods for astronauts are made extra spicy!

Bitter

Sour

Salty

Sweet

TASTE AREAS

Most of the 10,000 taste buds are on the tongue, though some are on the rear roof of the mouth and in the upper throat. It is thought that different parts of the tongue detect different flavours (left). The tip picks out sweet ones, the front sides salty ones, the rear sides sour ones, and the rear centre bitter flavours. The main upper surface of the tongue has few taste buds.

IN TOUCH

Your sense of touch is really an array of various types of contact senses. They include detection of light pressure, heavy pressure, fast or slow vibrations, temperature and also degrees of itching, soreness, discomfort and pain. These features are picked up by millions of different micro-sensors embedded just under the surface of your skin. They are specialised nerve endings and, as they change in shape with contact, or alter their temperature, they produce nerve signals.

The body's sensitivity to these different aspects of touch varies over its surface, depending on how many and what type of sensors are there. For example, the fingertips are very sensitive to light touch, but not especially to temperature.

22

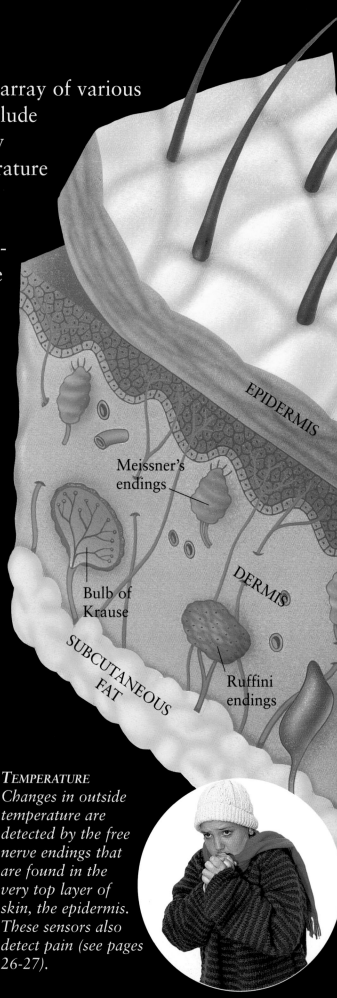

EPIDERMIS

Meissner's
endings

DERMIS

Bulb of
Krause

SUBCUTANEOUS
FAT

Ruffini
endings

THE SENSITIVE BODY
This touch-sensory figure (left) shows the relative sensitivity of the skin over different parts of the body. The lips, hands and fingers are very sensitive.

TEMPERATURE
Changes in outside temperature are detected by the free nerve endings that are found in the very top layer of skin, the epidermis. These sensors also detect pain (see pages 26-27).

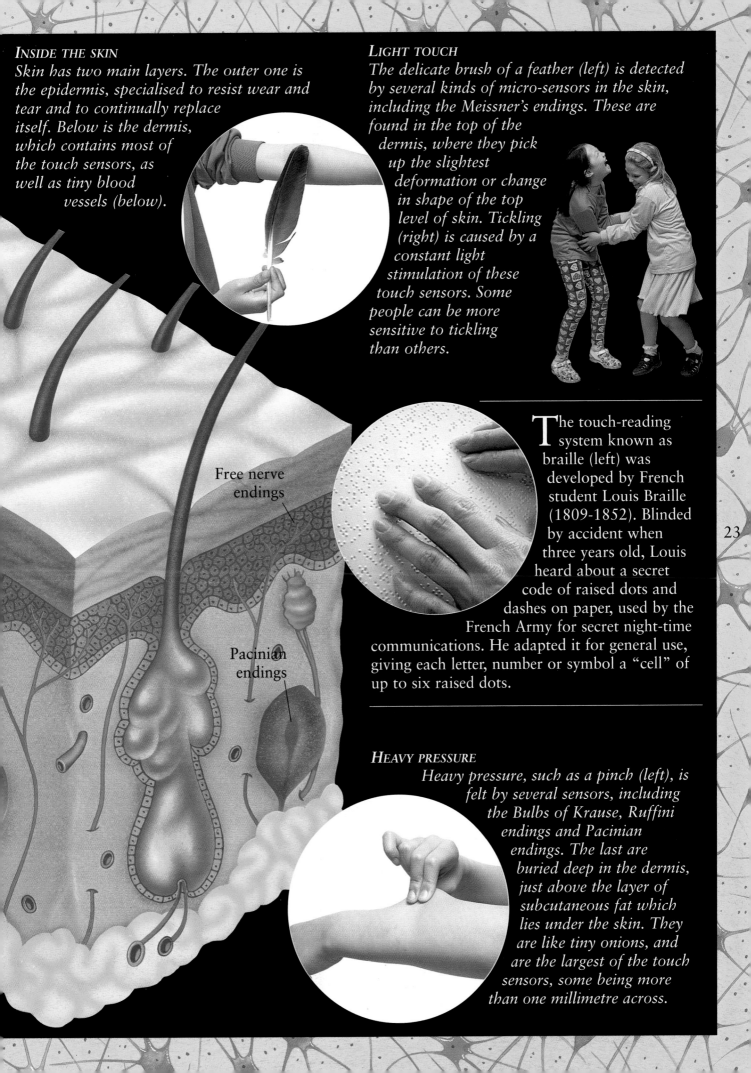

INSIDE THE SKIN

Skin has two main layers. The outer one is the epidermis, specialised to resist wear and tear and to continually replace itself. Below is the dermis, which contains most of the touch sensors, as well as tiny blood vessels (below).

LIGHT TOUCH

The delicate brush of a feather (left) is detected by several kinds of micro-sensors in the skin, including the Meissner's endings. These are found in the top of the dermis, where they pick up the slightest deformation or change in shape of the top level of skin. Tickling (right) is caused by a constant light stimulation of these touch sensors. Some people can be more sensitive to tickling than others.

Free nerve endings

Pacinian endings

The touch-reading system known as braille (left) was developed by French student Louis Braille (1809-1852). Blinded by accident when three years old, Louis heard about a secret code of raised dots and dashes on paper, used by the French Army for secret night-time communications. He adapted it for general use, giving each letter, number or symbol a "cell" of up to six raised dots.

23

HEAVY PRESSURE

Heavy pressure, such as a pinch (left), is felt by several sensors, including the Bulbs of Krause, Ruffini endings and Pacinian endings. The last are buried deep in the dermis, just above the layer of subcutaneous fat which lies under the skin. They are like tiny onions, and are the largest of the touch sensors, some being more than one millimetre across.

INNER SENSES

THE BODY HAS A MULTITUDE OF INNER SENSES. These include checking the levels of sugar in your blood and monitoring the positions of your limbs and your blood pressure. The last is monitored by pressure sensors in the walls of various arteries, especially the carotid artery in the neck. These sensors send signals to the brain which tells your heart to beat faster should the pressure drop and slower if it rises. Similarly, the brain sends signals to the kidneys, telling them to take more water out of the blood if the pressure rises, and take out less water if it drops (main picture).

HEAT CONTROL
The skin helps to control body temperature. A rise in core temperature is detected by heat-detecting cells in the brain. These start the process of sweating, the release of watery sweat onto the skin, which evaporates and cools the body (left). Alternatively, if the body becomes cold, the hairs on your skin are pulled upright to trap warm air near the skin (below).

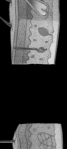

Upright hairs

CONTROL CONSOLE
Like your body, a complex machine, such as a car (below), has a central console where information is shown by screens and dials. This information comes from various sensors in the car.

BRAIN

CAROTID ARTERY

HEART

BLOOD PRESSURE
The force of blood inside the arteries is called blood pressure. A doctor can measure this, using a stethoscope and a device called a sphygmomanometer (above). With these, he or she can tell if your pressure is too high or low.

M ost tissues of the body use a type of sugar, glucose, as their basic energy source. This is obtained from digested food that you have eaten and travels around your body in the blood. After eating, glucose levels in the blood will rise. This increase is detected by chemical sensors in the brain. These sensors tell the body to produce chemicals called hormones, such as insulin. These hormones put any excess blood glucose into storage and bring levels back to normal.

Problems in this glucose feedback-and-control mechanism can lead to the condition called diabetes. Sufferers of this condition need to monitor the level of sugar in their blood carefully to ensure that it does not get too high. They may also require regular injections of insulin (below) to help keep the amount of sugar in their blood at a constant level.

SENSE OF TIME
Volunteers living for weeks in special rooms where the surroundings – light levels, temperature, sounds and so on – remain totally constant, still show a cycle of activity. They sleep, wake, rest, exercise and eat in a routine lasting about 24 hours. This is due to the body's own "clock" inside the brain, called the supra-chiasmatic nucleus. In the real world, environmental factors such as daylight, darkness and temperature changes, and our social cycle of work and rest govern this "body clock". In nature, the similar clocks of animals, such as squirrels, govern annual activity such as hibernation (below).

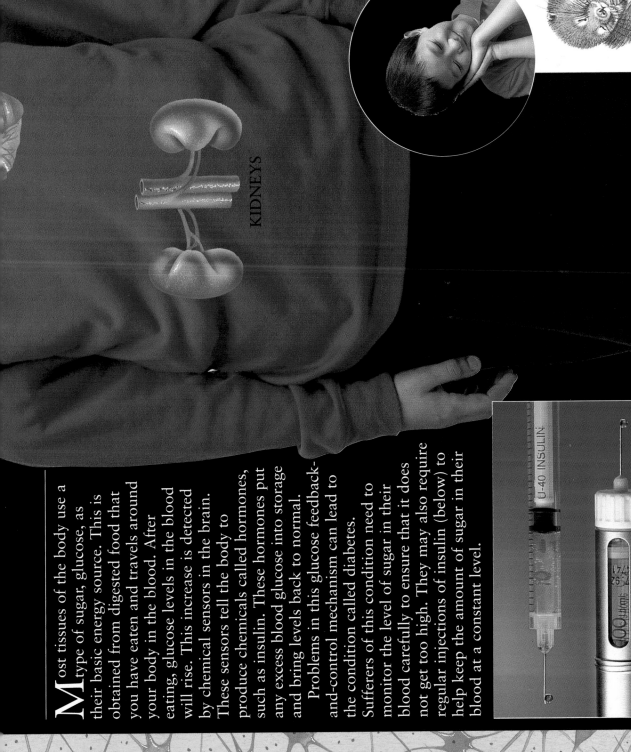

KIDNEYS

U-40 INSULIN

FEELING PAIN

WHEN YOU STUB your toe or bang your head, you might wish that the body lacked its sense of pain. But it is vital for survival. Pain warns you that the body is being harmed, and action is needed to get rid of the danger. Pain causes the body to make fast reflexes or movements called avoidance reactions. There are also pains which happen inside the body, indicating injury, pressure or disease.

Sometimes, athletes, such as long-distance runners (above right), run into the "pain barrier". This is when the body experiences so much pain that it feels that it cannot go on. When this happens, some athletes grit their teeth and continue running to take them through the "barrier".

Nerve

Pain signal

Synapse

Dendrite

MUSCLE

NERVE CELLS
Neurons carry nerve signals (right). Each has a cell body, projections called dendrites and a wire called the axon. The gap between nerves is called the synapse. Chemicals flood across this gap to the next neuron, to keep the signal going.

REFLEXES
A painful touch causes signals to go from the finger, along the arm to the spinal cord. Here, they are sent to the brain, making you aware of pain. But already a reflex arc in the spinal cord has sent signals back to the arm muscles to jerk the finger away.

Axon

Cell body

BRAIN

Nerve
signal
going to
muscle

SPINAL CORD

TYPES OF PAIN
*Pains can be described
in terms of their
characteristics – the
way they affect you.
The most common
terms include stabbing,
burning, crushing and
shooting (left).*

Stabbing

Burning

Crushing

Shooting

There are many ways of
reducing pain, including
drugs, such as analgesics,
which relieve pain and
anaesthetics, which totally
remove any feeling or
sensation. Some affect the
sensory cells and their nerves,
called the peripheral nervous
system. Others work on the central
nervous system, which
consists of the spinal
cord and the brain.

27

NATURAL PAIN BLOCKERS
*The body's own pain-control
system uses substances called
endorphins. These
act in the brain and
spinal cord to block
pain signals at
synapses between
neurons (left).
Endorphins are
released when the
body is active and
stressed, such as when
you are racing. This
lets you concentrate
on basic survival.*

TRICKING THE SENSES

THE NATURAL WORLD has green-winged butterflies who look like leaves, spotted cats and deer who blend in with the forest shadows, tiny shrews with loud shrill shrieks, flowers that smell of rotting meat and plants that resemble lumps of rock. These devices for disguise have evolved to trick the eyes, ears and other senses of creatures who might be predators.

In the human world, we use technology to recreate similar examples, such as advanced computers, TV screens and loudspeakers, and synthesising artificial substances in chemical laboratories. We can create a whole array of scenes, sounds, scents, tastes and feelings that fool our senses and trick our brain.

VISUAL ILLUSION
We can now make many unnatural scenes and patterns that trick our visual processing systems. Is this two faces or one candlestick (above)?

28

VIRTUAL REALITY
The VR (virtual reality) machine has small built-in screens for the eyes and headphone speakers for the ears (left). It may be accompanied by special motion-sensing gloves and a moving chair, to create a world that seems almost real –
yet it's entirely generated by computer. With it you can play incredibly realistic games or explore a long-ruined ancient temple.

NATURE'S SECRETS
Humans have copied animals' abilities to hide themselves against almost any background. Can you see a snake, a stick insect, a leaf insect, a chameleon, a frog and a spider in the picture (right)?

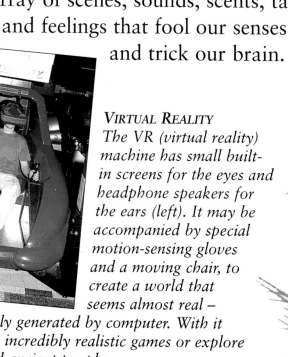

TASTES AND SMELLS
Humans can now make a wide variety of chemicals to mimic a range of flavours and scents (above).

MOVING PICTURES
Modern cinemas attempt to recreate life events as realistically as possible. They employ amazing special effects and stereo sound to make us believe we are really there. Other attempts have included 3-D films (left) and smell-o-vision!

PHANTOM LIMBS
If part of the body is removed, as with the British naval hero Nelson (right), the stump may still contain nerves that originally carried signals from the skin, muscles and joints of the removed part to the brain. These cut-off nerves may get stimulated. This leads to the sensations of a "phantom limb". The missing part feels as if it is still there.

3-D PATTERNS
The apparently random pattern (below), called an autostereogram, actually contains a three-dimensional picture hidden in its jumble of colours. Stare at the picture and unfocus your eyes, as if you were staring at an object far away. After time, the three-dimensional shape of a horse should emerge.

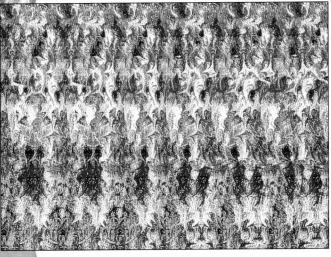

KNOW YOUR BODY!

IF YOU THOUGHT *humans had a good sense of smell, it is nothing compared to that of the male emperor moth (left). The aerial-like antennae on the head of this sensitive insect can detect the scent of a female emperor moth at the incredible range of 11 km (6.8 miles). The male then follows this delicate scent to track down the female over vast distances and mate with her.*

THE HUMAN EYE *is a small, marble-sized sphere, about 2.5 cm (1 inch) across (below). Compare this with the eye of the Atlantic giant squid, which has the largest eye of any animal, living or extinct. The eye of this huge 2-tonne monster measures about 40 cm (16 in) across! It uses this to see in the almost black depths where little sunlight reaches and the squid lives, some 2 km (1.25 miles) beneath the surface of the ocean.*

THE COLOURS *of the rainbow, from red to violet, show the complete range of colours that the human eye can detect. It is estimated that the eye can tell the difference between over 10 million different colours. However, visible light, that is the light you can see, forms only one seventieth, 1.5 per cent, of the entire electromagnetic· spectrum.*

YOUR NOSE *can smell over 10,000 different odours. To do this, it uses about 20 million smell cells found lining the nasal cavity. Some smells, such as musk sprays and skunk odours can be smelled at a concentration of one part in 20 billion!*

TIGHTROPE WALKING *(right) requires an amazing control of your balance. The endurance record for staying on a tightrope belongs to Jorge Ojeda-Guzman of the United States who spent 205 days balancing on a wire. During this time, he entertained crowds by balancing on a chair and dancing!*

An alternative balancing record was set by Girish Sharma of India, who stood on one foot for a total of 55 hours and 35 minutes. In this time, the airborne foot was not allowed to be rested on the other and no object could be used for support.

GLOSSARY

Ampullae – The bulges found in the semicircular canals of the inner ear, inside which are the cristae, that detect your body's movements.

Balance – The sense which helps you monitor the position of your body and keep it upright. It uses sensors in the ear and in muscles and joints around the body.

Binocular vision – The ability to see things in three dimensions using two points of vision, i.e. your two eyes.

Blood pressure – The force at which blood flows through your arteries.

Cochlea – The coiled organ found in the inner ear. It contains the sensory cells that detect sounds.

Cristae – The jelly-like lumps found inside the ampullae. They bend in response to movements of your body, creating nerve signals that are sent to the brain.

Decibels – The unit for measuring the intensity or loudness of sounds.

Diabetes – A disease in which there is too much glucose in the blood.

Electromagnetic spectrum – The total range of rays. It includes the light you can see – visible light – and rays you can't, including infra-red and ultraviolet light and X-rays.

Endorphins – Your body's natural pain killers. They block pain signals reaching the brain.

Focusing – The ability to create a sharp image.

Hearing – The sense which allows you to pick up sounds, using the ears.

Hertz – The unit of frequency. It tells you the number of times a sound wave vibrates each second.

Neurons – The cells that carry nerve signals around your body.

Olfactory epithelium – The layer that lines the roof of your nasal cavity and holds the smell cells.

Optic nerve – The nerve that carries visual signals from the eye to the brain.

Papillae – The tiny, pimple-like bumps that cover the surface of your tongue.

Parallax – The relative sizes and positions of objects as they become smaller with distance.

Proprioceptors – The sensors found in muscles, tendons and joints which tell the brain the position of the body.

Reflex – A reaction that does not involve a decision that you are aware of.

Semicircular canals – The C-shaped tubes found in the inner ear that help detect movement.

Senses – The general term given to the faculties that allow you to monitor what's going on inside your body and the outside world.

Sight – The sense that lets you see the world around you, using your eyes.

Smell – The sense that allows you to experience odours, using smell cells in the roof of the nasal cavity.

Taste – The sense that lets you experience flavours, using taste buds on the tongue and upper throat.

Touch – The sense that allows you to feel the world around you. The majority of touch sensors are found in the skin. They detect heat, pressure and vibrations.

Vitreous humor – The clear jelly that fills the inside of the eyeball.

INDEX

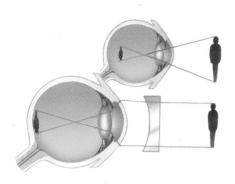

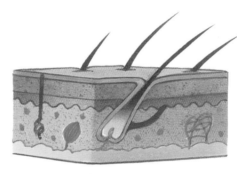

Photo credits:
Abbreviations: t-top, m-middle, b-bottom, r-right, l-left

Cover ml, 5t, 8t, 10, 11tl & m, 15t, 20t, 23m, 24b, 25b & 27b – Science Photo Library. Cover m, 3tr & b, 6 all, 7 all, 8b, 9 all, 11tr & b, 12t, 13 both, 14, 19 all, 20b, 20-21, 22, 23t & b, 24tl, 24-25, 25t, 26b, 26-27, 28, 29tl, 30mr & bl – Roger Vlitos. 3tl & 16 – Spectrum Colour Library. 5m, 17br, 30t & ml – Bruce Coleman Collection. 12m & 17bl – Eye Ubiquitous. 17t & 29tr – Rex Features. 17m, 18, 21, 26t & 29b – Frank Spooner Pictures. 24tr Courtesy Rolls Royce Motor Cars/Vickers PLC. 29m & 30br – Mary Evans Picture Library.